I0707448

Preface To Kuwait, Qatar, And Israel

While I did serve in the U.S. Army, I did not see combat. I say again, I did not see combat. In fact, the highlight of my Army career was a year-long deployment in Kuwait in support of Operation Iraqi Freedom as an Administrative Specialist who typed on a computer all day. While in Kuwait, I visited Qatar, and after my Kuwait deployment, I went on a religious mission to Israel. After all of this, I finished my Bachelor's Degree in Political Science and worked several civilian jobs. I will spend most of this book speaking about my time in Kuwait, Qatar, and Israel, and how that shaped my views on Middle East Peace.

Chapter 1: Enlisting In The U.S. Army

When I was very young, my family bought me a book about ancient Egypt. I was fascinated by the history in it. The story of the Egyptian Dynasties, the stories of the Pharaohs, and the stories of the Pyramids inspired me. I did not know that several decades later, when I was all grown up, that the Middle East would become my number one passion in life. I will now flash forward to my High School days. In the 2002-2003 school year, towards the end of High School, I went to my gym teacher, a man whom to this day I have great respect for, and told him I want to prepare for the Army. He told me I should wrestle.

The workouts were difficult, and I lost a lot of weight; I went down from 200 lbs. all the way to 152 lbs. at one point. I got to meet a lot of good people on the team and I even got to wrestle at two tournaments. My school had one of the greatest Wrestling teams in my state. Thank goodness I decided to wrestle before I joined the Army as Basic Combat Training would be the most grueling physical training I have ever done in my life to this day. And wrestling definitely prepared me for that and got me in good shape.

During the first Wrestling tournament, I wrestled a 6'3" inch tall white gentleman with blonde hair and blue eyes. His hair was long, about almost up to the shoulders and very curly. We wrestled at 171 lbs., even though the gentleman was much taller and much bigger than me. I am only 5'7". I was not too nervous though. I was just thinking, *I am going to stay in this thing as long as I can. I am not going for the pin but I am going to wrestle for as long as I can.* When the whistle was blown, I came in very quickly and locked up with one arm around his shoulder and the other arm around the back of his neck.

I was very inexperienced, so my tactic was to try to scare him. In hindsight, it was a bad idea to try to scare someone who is 6'3" and 171 lbs. of solid muscle. I began to push and pull him again and again in an effort to both off-balance and intimidate him. Then I went for a single leg. A single leg in Wrestling is when you move forward and bend down a little and grab one leg of the opponent. You then either trip his other leg with your own leg or you go for what is known as a double leg. A double leg is when you grab one leg and then grab the second leg and go down with him. Note that in Folkstyle High School Wrestling, you cannot throw your opponent to the floor without going down with him to secure his landing, because that would be known as a slam.

Anyhow, he ended up doing a body lock on me. A move that I have not learned yet. I tried to bend down slightly and shoot for his leg (move quickly towards him and then slide on one knee in his direction). He grabbed me in a type of bear hug from the front and then transitioned to standing behind me while still holding me and tossed me and went down with me of course to secure my landing. But it felt like the black rubber mat was made out of concrete when I hit it. He even took the wind out of me when I hit the mat and I remember my wrestling singlet, a one piece wrestling uniform that we wore with special wrestling shoes, being covered completely in sweat within two to three seconds of me hitting the mat. His arms were still wrapped around me and he was holding his hands tightly together around my stomach area. I grabbed for his hands and tried to pry them off, but then, using his superior strength and technique, he proceeded to put me on the mat on my back and pin me and I struggled at first, but his hold was so strong that I eventually gave up and just laid there until the referee blew the whistle. Afterwards, we all went through a line (one team made one line and the other team made another line) and we went by and thanked each other. Either the gentleman I wrestled or someone that looks very similar to him, stated to me, as he shook my hand, "Way to wrestle." He knew I had heart.

The 2nd gentleman I wrestled was a white gentleman, with a blonde buzz cut, weighed about 152 lbs. and was about 5'6", an inch shorter than me. This was at my 2nd Wrestling tournament, a few weeks later. Even though the gentleman was an inch shorter than me, my one inch height advantage was negated by the fact that I lost so much weight to compete against him. At 171 lbs., I had already learned my lesson to not wrestle guys who are too heavy for me, as their muscle overrides my fat. So coming in this time at 152 lbs., I did a little bit better. I got out of some of his holds, which surprised me as he was very fast, and I lasted into the 2nd round, but he eventually pinned me. While not as strong as my previous opponent, he felt twice as fast. At the Wrestling tournaments, I lost both matches that I wrestled but I, and everyone else on the team, knew I had heart. This heart I would need to make it through Army Basic Training.

I graduated from High School in May of 2003 and enlisted in the U.S. Army Reserve. After attending a few drills with my Army Reserve unit, whom would become some of the greatest people I've ever known, I attended Basic Combat Training at Ft. Jackson, South Carolina. I left for Basic Combat Training on November 4th, 2003. The Drill Sergeants were hard but fair. They were also some of the greatest people I've ever known. I want to get this off my chest. My scariest moments were Victory Tower and the Confidence Course.

I am scared of heights. I remember being told by my fellow recruits to have discipline and look straight ahead while getting ready to go up Victory Tower, a 30 foot massive behemoth, complete with a repelling wall, a ropes course, and a cargo net. They told me this as per the instructions of the Drill Sergeants there. We were to stand at attention while waiting in line, but I was so scared that I could not help but look up at the looming tower. I went up and down the tower, went through the ropes course, and went down the cargo net. I did all these things, but I forgot which order I did them in. It wasn't as scary as I thought it would be, but scary nonetheless.

My second scariest moment was the Confidence Course. I remember being really scared going up the giant ladder, which, like Victory Tower, was also 30 feet high. I was scared, but once again, I did it. That is all I remember from the Confidence Course, other than the fact that it rained and we had to cancel the rest of the course after I completed about half of it. I am sure glad that I made it through both Victory Tower and The Confidence Course, I consider those two events in particular, and making it through Basic Combat Training in general, two of some of my biggest accomplishments in life.

Another event that I remember was the Gas Chamber. I remember being told before going to Basic Training by some Veterans and Active Duty military alike to not shave beforehand and to not eat the Chili Mac that the Drill Sergeants will offer you. I enjoyed some of the food that the Drill Sergeants served us but I did not eat the Chili Mac as it was not a requirement but I did shave beforehand, as I consider myself very "Hooah!" Hooah is a word in the Army that means everything but 'no'. As we lined up in the Gas Chamber, around the Dragon (the cauldron that emitted the CS Gas), I remembered that we were told by the Drill Sergeant to not touch the Dragon. By this point, we were all wearing our Protective Masks.

In the Army, you call them Protective Masks and not Gas Masks; this was a requirement just as calling your rifle a weapon and not a gun was also a requirement. The Drill Sergeants were obviously wearing the Protective Masks too as they came into the Gas Chamber well before we did. Then we were told to take our hand and put it on the lower part of our masks and move them up, just enough to inhale some CS gas, say Name, Rank, and Social Security Number, as well as sing The Army Song. I said all this in between screaming from the pain of the CS getting into the pores of my face. Everyone else tended to cough a lot. I regretted shaving that morning.

After singing and saying my pertinent data, we were told to put the bottom part of the masks back on and clear and seal the masks. I cleared the mask with my right hand while breathing out and then I put my left hand on the filter and breathed in until the mask stuck to my face. I then released my left hand and the mask unstuck from my face. You know your mask is sealed when putting your hand on the filter and breathing in makes the mask stick to your face. We were then told to remove our masks completely, sing The Army Song, and then leave the Gas Chamber. As scary as the Gas Chamber is for some recruits, it was not scary for me as being in an enclosed environment low to the ground means I won't have to deal with heights, one of my biggest fears, and my only irrational phobia.

I must apologize for discussing my Basic Training experience in an out of order fashion as I am remembering the most interesting parts first. On the Rifle Qualification Range, on my 2nd attempt, I made Marksman. While the lowest qualification score, I was happy with it as I made the standard and was on my way to graduate Basic Training. My biggest challenge, passing the Two-Mile Run in under sixteen minutes and thirty six seconds, was yet to come.

My favorite part of Basic Combat Training was the Anzio Range, named after a World War II Battle that took place in Italy. We went navigating through pitch black, at nighttime, and I could barely see, and eventually all of us (the recruits) got to a set of metal pole stakes towards the end of the course. Each set of stakes contained two stakes, one on each side of the recruit's weapon. They were placed in sectors of fire. A sector of fire is where a Soldier is ordered to visually scan the landscape/terrain in front of him/her, and if need be, fire his/her weapon at the enemy.

As I got to my sector of fire, I got in the prone position and readied my M16A2 rifle. I took it off Safe and put it on Semi and began to fire. I neglected to mention that we had tracer rounds in our magazine. So, I don't remember exactly if every round was a tracer round, or if every third or fourth round was a tracer round, but our M16 rifles lit up the night. They looked like short laser beams from science fiction movies. Not only did I experience awe that night, I also achieved my training objectives for the evening.

Chapter 2: The Dreaded 2 Mile Run And Victory Forge

On the day of the 2 Mile Run, my Drill Sergeant had one of the most high speed (quick-learning) and squared away (knows what needs to be done and how to do it) Soldiers run alongside with me. I passed the Pushups and Situps on the APFT (Army Physical Fitness Test) with no problems. Then as I ran, even at sea level at Ft. Jackson, I remember screaming from the pain in my chest and pain in my legs as I have never ran so hard in my life. The recruit, a six foot two inch tall blonde gentleman with blue eyes, who was wearing a gray Army PT (physical training) T-shirt and black Army shorts, white socks, and white sneakers, as was I, ran alongside me.

The Drill Sergeant who was watching our progress stood near the middle of the oval-shaped track we were running on. We were running outdoors. During the test, I could hear various music from 70's, 80's, and 90's action and sports movies playing to get us pumped up. I ran hard and fast, sometimes screaming as loud as I can. This was both from the pain and to open up my diaphragm and increase my rate of breathing. Running as hard and as fast as I could, I managed to pass the test in 15:48; the required test time minimum was 16:36. I barely made it, but what mattered was that I *did* make it.

The next day came Victory Forge. We put on our BDUs (Battle Dress Uniforms), what civilians call green woodland camouflage uniforms. We got our LBV (load-bearing vests) on. The LBV is basically a green vest that goes over the uniform that carries a first aid pouch and pouches for extra magazines for the M16 rifle. We also put on our Kevlar helmets. The Kevlar helmets had bands that we put in to make wearing them more comfortable, nevertheless it became uncomfortable very quickly during the march as both the headband became tight and the helmet became heavy. We also wore a rucksack which carried additional gear. I remember the 1st generation rucksacks being hard to tie up after we filled them up and being almost as hard to put on. We carried our M16 rifles during the 10 mile march.

Marching was easy as I am a good walker, but not a good runner. I made it all 10 miles to the site of Victory Forge, our FTX (Field Training Exercise), without getting tired. I was moving so fast and it came so naturally and easily for me that my Drill Sergeant said something to me I thought I would never hear, "Slow down." Even the high speed gentleman that helped me run said he never thought that he would hear the Drill Sergeant say that.

The site of Victory Forge was a heavily wooded area of Ft. Jackson. It looked like it was straight out of a World War II movie. We began to dig our trenches. I do not remember if we used actual shovels, an entrenching tool, or both, but we dug and dug, and after about a day, my Battle Buddy and I had dug a two person trench, as had everyone else in our Basic Training Platoon (a platoon is a 30 person unit). An entrenching tool is like a sharp small shovel that can either dig a trench or be used to attack an enemy, much like a bayonet. A battle buddy is a person who is part of your two person team in Basic Training. You never go anywhere without a battle buddy, who is always your same rank (I was a Private at the time). We also had two person tents that we set up.

The fact that my Basic Training was in the winter time was both a blessing and a curse. A blessing in that it was very unusually cold and easy to run and march in, but a curse in that I only slept one hour in all of the seventy-two hours we were out there at Victory Forge, because of the cold. We finished digging our trenches during the day, and at night came our first simulated enemy attack during Victory Forge. A flare shot up in the sky and the night, for several seconds, became illuminated almost like daytime. We heard blank ammunition going off and several CS grenades were thrown towards us. So we naturally put on our protective masks and yelled, "Gas! Gas! Gas!" We stood in our trenches, waiting for the simulated enemy attack. Then came the CS grenades. It's amazing, I was coughing until I put on my mask, but the Drill Sergeants were walking around without masks and the CS did not seem to affect them. At one point, one of the Drill Sergeants commented that my weapon (M16A2 rifle) was frosted over when he came over to inspect our trench after the simulated gas attack.

After two and a half days, we started the long march back. Back in the Barracks, I was so tired from only sleeping one hour during that whole period that I felt refreshed after sleeping four to five hours in the Barracks. The next day was graduation. We got in our Class A uniforms (that is a Green Military Dress Suit uniform) and attended graduation. We heard the Colonel and then General speak and we sang the Army Song. Basic Training was hard but I do miss my Drill Sergeants and feel that it was one of my favorite times of my life. I got my Orders for AIT (Advanced Individualized Training, or job training), in the front leaning rest (pushup) position.

Chapter 3: AIT

This will be a short chapter as I call this next part Basic Training Lite. Since my MOS (Military Occupational Specialty) was as an Administrative Specialist, a support MOS with training at Ft. Jackson, I did not have to go far for AIT (Advanced Individualized Training). We got on a bus and were bussed from one part of the base to another. Our Drill Sergeants and the Sergeants that trained us for our MOS at AIT were more relaxed and I felt less jacked up (more able to handle this and not as physically slow as I was in Basic Training). It really helped that my High School Business teacher taught me how to type home row. I ended up typing over 80 words per minute in High School. This only helped me at

AIT. We did a lot of typing of reports and we concluded with a field exercise, with a slightly shorter march and slightly shorter time in the field. Thankfully, AIT was very easy and like I said in the beginning of the chapter, it was basically Basic Training Lite.

I was glad it was easier with less marching and less time in the field as we were in the month of February at AIT and it was starting to get hot in South Carolina. So maybe it was a blessing in disguise that it was unusually cold when I got to Basic Combat Training. After I completed my Admin training, this was now early 2004, I got back to my unit and spent some time stationed on a base on active duty stateside. Then after I finished my stateside tour, I went to University concurrently with my Army Reserve training. I studied Political Science. After a year of school, I got called up to Active Duty again. This time to Kuwait.

Chapter 4: Kuwait

Around August of 2005, my unit and I arrived at Ft. Bliss, Texas. We then did three months of training before deploying to Kuwait. I remember we had convoy training. Lots and lots of convoy training with Humvees. After we finished training and got our paperwork squared away, we boarded a plane and after what seemed like half a day of flying, landed in Kuwait. We landed in Kuwait on

November 4th, 2005. This was coincidentally two years to the day that I left for Basic Training. After we arrived on base, it felt very cool and nice. Not too hot and not too cold. We stayed in temporary housing tents that fit about ten people each for the first several weeks of our deployment. Then we were moved to our trailers that we would call home for the rest of the deployment. After a few months on base, the contractors on base turned on the AC. We were complaining for two days that it was too cold and that they turned on the AC too early. We would soon realize how wrong we were too complain as soon the temperature got up to 110 Degrees Fahrenheit, and eventually, in June, July, and August of 2006, the temperature got up to 127 Degrees Fahrenheit in the shaded area, even though all our thermometers actually read 140 Degrees and over in Fahrenheit. I will not spend any more time talking about what I did military-wise in Kuwait, other than I did Admin work, but I will tell you about life there and the people and their beautiful culture that I experienced.

I remember visiting Kuwait City. They have a beautiful pier there that overlooks antique boats. They have a cultural center there too. There were several beautiful skyscrapers there as well. Most of the country is contrasted with two story tall buildings made out of concrete. Only Kuwait City, as far as I know, had the skyscrapers. This is similar to Israel, in how Tel Aviv has many skyscrapers and West Jerusalem has several skyscrapers, but the rest of the country has smaller buildings. But I will get into Israel in the chapter after the next one. I remember eating at a Kuwaiti restaurant. We ate a marvelous rice dish and the servers and hosts were very pleasant, warm, and friendly.

The animal life was beautiful too, and in my mind, very unique. When I went to a museum/zoo in Kuwait City, the cats were tan and had pointed ears like the elves from early folklore. The rats had forward bent knees and jump up and down like kangaroos, hence their name, kangaroo rats. There were camels, and then there were scorpions and camel spiders. The camel spider is like a large tan-colored and very hairy spider, but not poisonous, at least, I don't think. The scorpions are the ones that people should worry about. But like we were told stateside when several Soldiers inquired about mosquitos, there are no mosquitos in the Middle East. Thank goodness. But there are locusts.

And I remember in the fall (both in November 2005 and October 2006), on base, we had literally a Biblical-proportion plague of locusts. I was literally walking around one time and I had hundreds of locusts all over me and all around me, but they seemed, and were, very harmless. The sight of them was more beautiful than anything else. Also on base, I remember there were entire weeks when we would see a giant blood orange moon. I don't know why it was so big, but it looked three or four times bigger than what the moon looks like back home in the United States. Looking back on it now, I am thinking that the Kuwaiti moonlight should be called one of the wonders of the world.

And then, then came the dreaded PT Test again. This was sometime in mid-2006, don't remember when exactly. This time, I had to make it in 15:54. I was a Private First Class at the time. A Staff Sergeant with my unit, a 5'7" black gentleman, who had a slight accent, and was always ready to help anyone who ever needed it, ran alongside me. I have a slight accent too, being originally from Ukraine. He kept yelling at me to, "Hurry up. Get here. Get right here!" and he pointed to where he wanted me to be at. I struggled to keep up, I ran so fast, and screamed and yelled and was in so much pain. But I had to keep up. *I cannot let myself fail*, I thought.

I was told after the test ended, in which I ran a 15:50 and passed, that I kept up with one of the fastest people in the unit, a gentleman originally from Belarus. One gentleman in my unit even commented that he thought I was a monster coming to eat him when I was running because I was yelling so much. I guess I do have heart. I then got my promotion to my final rank of Specialist. A Specialist is the same pay grade as Corporal, but with less command responsibility. That became one of my proudest achievements in the Army. I will always remember what that Staff Sergeant did for me to make this happen. After the PT Test, came my R&R pass to Qatar. I had so much fun in Qatar.

Chapter 5: Qatar

This, the R&R Pass to Qatar, was also in mid-2006, like the PT Test. On my 4 day R&R pass, I stayed on a really cool base in Qatar. We had pizza, three beers a day, and TV. I normally don't drink, I drink hardly ever, but I did end up having three beers a day every night. On the first day, I went off-roading with several other Soldiers in an SUV. The Qatari driver took us up to the top of the sand dunes, one sand dune at a time, obviously, and then took us straight down. It was very fast and very cool. I even have grainy video of us going down the sand dunes to this day. On the second day, I went to several restaurants.

The people who served us were very nice and very friendly. At one restaurant, which overlooked the Persian Gulf, the gentleman who owned it, said many people go to this restaurant from all over the Middle East. Some that go are Syrian, some Palestinian, and some are Jordanian, among others. I remember going to a Hookah bar in Qatar and smoking tobacco through a Hookah pipe. I am a tobacco user, both smoker and chewer, so I loved the Hookah bar. Then I went with several other Soldiers to the beach. Now I can say to people I've been to the Persian Gulf.

On the third day, I went to the mall. I met a very friendly Egyptian gentleman that really hooked me up. He showed me around the mall and even let me smoke cigarettes with him, even indoors! That used to be legal here in the United States but now, unfortunately for me, it is now illegal. Smoking sections of restaurants are now nonexistent. He showed me some of the shops, where the local shopkeepers were so nice. I purchased several Egyptian-style pyramids made out of stone, about hand-held sized. I purchased a scorpion and camel spider encased in acrylic. I also purchased several Russian-style Matryoshka dolls. The Matryoshka dolls were especially cool, since I'm originally from Ukraine, they remind me of my heritage.

I remember feeling very sad that I did not take many pictures of my time in Qatar. When the Egyptian gentleman I was with asked me why I looked sad, I stated that I did not have anything to remember this place by. So he took pictures of me with Hookah pipes at the Hookah store, he took pictures of me with paintings, and he took pictures of me with Egyptian statues that were in the mall.

I just remembered that I have pictures of myself with a red hat with a tassel on it, called a Fez. The gentleman I spoke of took those pictures too. I don't know the origin of it, but it could be generally Middle Eastern or specifically Moroccan, I am not sure though. We even listened to Rap and R&B music together. I miss hanging out with him. On the fourth day in Qatar, I remember having my three beers, ordering a large pizza, and watching a horror movie on TV. I must have ate that entire pizza in less than five minutes because I was so hungry. After I got back from Qatar to Kuwait, our deployment was wrapping up.

Chapter 6: Heading Home

In October of 2006, as the bus was leaving the base, and was taking us to the airport, a tear welled up in my eye as I would miss everyone that I worked with, the U.S. Military Servicemembers and the contractors. Our plane left Kuwait and after several stops in Europe, we landed stateside. Back home, my family was very happy to see me. I was happy to see them too. I spent almost twelve months deployed in Kuwait.

I was back on Reserve status after my deployment. I then started finishing up my University studies in Political Science. We were scheduled to do Annual Training in California, but I asked my Sergeant, Staff Sergeant, and Commander (a Captain at the time) if I could instead go on a Jewish religious mission to Israel, which my family had planned. The Commander authorized it. So now, I am back home, in school full-time, and planning a trip to Israel.

Chapter 7: Israel

I attended a Jewish religious mission in Israel in the summer of 2007. We landed in Tel Aviv and our tour guides picked us up, along with them, was a Rabbi. I am remembering now that we once went on a tour of King Solomon's aqueducts in East Jerusalem. We were underground and there was water up to our knees. It was fun though and it was an honor to do it. We prayed at the Wailing Wall, also in East Jerusalem. While I am secular now, I definitely remember feeling a tie to God and His presence when I was putting my note in the wall and saying a prayer as well. We went hiking a lot. We hiked on the Golan Heights one time. It was beautiful seeing the true beauty of nature. I have never hiked before until I visited Israel. When we visited Tel Aviv, I saw how different it looked from the rest of Israel. It had a bunch of steel skyscrapers while the rest of the country had concrete buildings. Very similar to how Kuwait had many concrete buildings and Kuwait City had a bunch of steel skyscrapers.

We went to several bars in Tel Aviv and after one or two nights of hiking and going sightseeing, I stopped going to bars and drinking. Even after two shots of Vodka, I felt too tired to go hiking and traveling the next day, but did so anyway, and to keep from being tired anymore while doing it, I just stayed in my hotel room at nighttime. By the way, in Israel a shot of Vodka is known as a chaser of Vodka, and two shots of Vodka are known as a shot of Vodka, if that makes sense. While in my hotel room, I listened to Israeli Hip Hop, Rock, R&B, Pop, and Mizrahi music that I purchased at the mall when we went to the mall in Tel Aviv. Israeli Mizrahi music, Mizrahi meaning 'Eastern' in Hebrew, sounds like Arabic music. In fact, many people who don't speak Arabic or Hebrew cannot distinguish Israeli or Arabic music from each other. That is how similar they are. I will speak of further cultural similarities between Israeli people and Arab people in future chapters.

My favorite experience, next to the Wailing Wall, of course, was going up the Fortress of Masada. You can see much of Israel from the top of there. The Masada Fortress was where a group of Ancient Israelites ran upon each other's swords rather than surrender to the invading Romans. Another equally favorite experience, just as good as seeing Masada, was spending the night at a Bedouin tent. The Bedouins are a group of nomadic Arabs who live in Israel. They gave us tea and food and let us stay in their tent for a night. They are a very humble and generous people. At one point during our trip in Israel, we even got to ride camels. I've ridden them before, stateside, at a Medieval Festival, but it is so much more powerful when you do it in the Middle East.

Chapter 8: My Future Plans

After I returned home from Israel, I gave my family some Israeli music CDs that I bought in Israel. You see, I bought multiple copies, some for myself, and some for family. By the way, just as Hebrew and Arabic are written right to left, Israeli music CD cases open in the opposite direction too. I then finished up my Bachelor's Degree in Political Science at University and finished up my military service with the U.S. Army Reserve, both in 2008. I worked several civilian jobs, from 2010-2018, and like in the military, the civilians I worked with became like family too, after several years of working with them. At University, like in Kuwait, Qatar, and Israel, I met many Jewish and Israeli students and professors, as well as Palestinian students and professors. They were very nice. At my civilian jobs, I have met several Israeli and Palestinian customers and employees who were equally as kind as those that I met at University.

Now I want to speak about what I want to do with my life next. I know it sounds like an ambitious goal, but I want to make the world a better place. I may make it a career in helping to shape the Middle East for a brighter future, but for now, I want this book to help the reader see what I think should happen in the Middle East. With my life experience in the Military, having served in Kuwait and having visited Qatar, and with my Jewish religious mission in Israel, and with my Political Science Degree, I know that I pretty much have a calling to work towards a better Middle East.

Chapter 9: A Top-Down Approach To Middle East Peace

Governments in Israel and in the Arab World are currently working toward Middle East Peace. We have heard of the One State Solution. In the One State Solution, we would have one state encompassing the whole Israeli-Palestinian peninsula for both the Israelis and Palestinians. We have heard of the Two-State Solution. The Two-State Solution involves Gaza and the West Bank becoming part of Palestine while pre-1967 Israel would stay as part of Israel. This is all good. As I write this, Saudi Arabia and Israel are developing a closer relationship in dealing with common security issues. The Israelis and Palestinians work in the Jordan Valley together on water rights, as well as on economic issues that affect both their peoples throughout the Israeli-Palestinian peninsula. Again, this is all good.

Governments need to continue to work for Middle East Peace. The U.N. and the U.S. should stay involved in the Middle East Peace Process as well. This is all working towards a good goal. But this is only the Top-Down Approach to Middle East Peace. I recommend, in addition to the Top-Down Approach, a Bottom-Up Approach to Middle East Peace.

Chapter 10: A Bottom-Up Approach To Middle East Peace

As I said in Chapter 8, my Kuwait deployment and my trip to Israel, as well as studying Political Science at University, has made me passionate about the Middle East and helping the people living there. In Kuwait and Qatar, as well as during my stay at the Bedouin tent in Israel, I learned first-hand about the friendliness and hospitality of the Arab people. They were willing to help me out when I needed help by taking photographs of me in Qatar when I had very few deployment photographs. They offered me free food and drink. And they took me on tours and listened to music with me. The Israeli people were equally kind. They taught me about Israeli culture and taught me about my Jewish heritage and took me all over the country to see what Israel is like.

I feel that, like how Governments work together for Middle East Peace, the people should work together for Middle East Peace too. As the people of Kuwait, Qatar, and Israel have been kind to me, I feel I need to repay that kindness by helping foster peace. For the remainder of this book, I will focus on the Israeli-Palestinian Peace Process for two reasons. 1.) It is very crucial to the entire region. And 2.) I studied it the most while in University.

In the United States, there are probably a hundred to two hundred Middle East Peace NGOs and Nonprofit Groups. And maybe ten to twenty large Middle East Peace NGOs and Nonprofit Groups functioning as umbrella organizations. I feel that there should be a thousand to five thousand Middle East Peace NGOs and Nonprofit Groups and maybe two hundred to three hundred large umbrella Middle East Peace NGOs and Nonprofit Groups.

In Israel and as well as in Kuwait and Qatar, I saw that both the Jewish People and the Arab People all have the same mannerisms. They all have the same hand gestures. They all have the same facial mannerisms. They even have a very similar inflection in language and speaking. They both speak Semitic languages (Arabic and Hebrew). Like I said earlier in the book, Arabic music and Israeli Mizrahi (Eastern) music both sound similar. And about half of classical Jewish music, if not more than half, sounds just as Middle Eastern as Arabic music. They both worship the same God as well.

We need to bring regular, everyday people from Israel and Palestine together on a massive scale the way we bring the Governments together. I know creating more NGOs costs money, but at the same time, if we give people the chance to see they have more in common than they thought, then I feel that this financial price is a price worth paying. If everyone in the Middle East just took a day of their lives to meet someone who is slightly different than them in some ways, but very similar in others, and took the time to talk to them, they would see that they are brothers and sisters and not adversaries.

Like I said before, in addition to Governments working together for peace, another commonly neglected path to peace is to have the people come together and talk. This is what is now needed to supplement the Peace Process. And hopefully, it will supplement the Peace Process to a great extent. Also, I have to note, in addition to finding common ground between Israelis and Palestinians, I always challenge myself to find one thing that I and somebody else like. Everyone is passionate about at least one thing that someone else that may be somehow different than them may be equally passionate about. That is what I strive for. And that is what we need to strive for in making peace.

Chapter 11: The Best Of Both Worlds And Finding One Commonality

Having introduced my bottom-up approach to peace, and having spoken of the already existing top-down approach to peace, I feel that it is critical for peace to succeed by having what I call the best of both worlds approach to peace. We need to have Middle Eastern Governments continue to have security cooperation and financial cooperation. But the people need to speak to each other too. That is why I think in the Middle East and in the United States, both the private sector and the government (Federal, State, and Local) should encourage the growth of more peace NGOs and Nonprofits by simply speaking about them. The funding will come later as more people decide to speak out by speaking to each other. When people see there is a demand for more peace and development organizations, then the funding will come.

When these new NGOs bring people together, even if the people meeting feel they have too many differences, the NGO should speak to them about finding one thing they are both passionate about. This one thing is what will unite those two individuals in their new bond. They will then not only help bring about Middle East Peace but will also use that one thing they have in common to create change for the better in other ways as well. This one commonality approach can bring about Middle East Peace from the bottom up, with some help from the top down. Governments will continue to negotiate and people will continue to speak with each other, and within a decade or so, we may very well have a lasting peace.

Chapter 12: The Committee Of Commonalities

Whether one supports a One State Solution or a Two-State Solution, I do not believe that the Israeli-Palestinian conflict is unsolvable. We as a society have been looking at the differences between Israelis and Palestinians, both politically and culturally, for decades now, and we should start looking at the similarities. The U.S. Government, the U.N., NATO Countries, the Arab League, and the Israelis and Palestinians should work together to create a joint Israeli-Palestinian Committee Of Commonalities. This committee will be staffed by both

Israelis and Palestinians. They will do research on what common cultural and political interests both sides have. They will then use this to create a just Israeli-Palestinian peace.

The Committee Of Commonalities will be staffed by both Government Officials and Private Citizens, thus combining the top down and bottom up approach. It will host foreign dignitaries who will advise the Israelis and Palestinians on how to adapt the security procedures of their own countries to Israel and Palestine, and guest speakers such as U.S. Military Active Duty and Veterans (both Officers and Enlisted) will further advise the Committee Of Commonalities as to security procedures. Everyday Israelis and Palestinians will advise The Committee Of Commonalities of the cultural sensitivities of both sides and both sides will learn to value and respect those sensitivities. Political Members of The Committee Of Commonalities will map out a just peace that both sides can agree with based on both differences and similarities, with the key focus being similarities.

Chapter 13: The NGOs Of Commonalities

Just as we should have an Israeli-Palestinian Committee Of Commonalities in the Government sphere that will combine both private citizens and government officials, we should also have NGOs that work on commonalities on the ground level. We already have NGOs in the United States that bring Israelis and Palestinians together, and this is good. I support expanding this. Like I said earlier in this book, by twice as much, three times as much, or even ten times as much. We need Israelis and Palestinians to meet more often. More private individuals meeting and speaking of peaceful brotherhood and sisterhood will allow for them to make change for the better. We need to create NGOs of Commonalities as well. By speaking out about their commonalities, Israelis and Palestinians can help bring about peace. Many Israelis and Palestinians that meet may like the same type of music. They may like Mixed Martial Arts. They may like Science Fiction. Whatever their hobbies, dreams, goals, they (Israelis and Palestinians) can learn to pursue them together.

While working together at the NGO level, to meet as friends and to speak to each other, and discuss their commonalities, or at least one big commonality, they can help bring about change at the local level, and eventually, they can petition the Israeli and Palestinian Governments, as well as the U.S. Government, of the necessary needs for change. The people should speak to the government and the government should then speak to the people. This way, everyone's views will be heard and not just the elite or those in political power. By speaking to each other, these NGOs of Commonalities and the Israeli-Palestinian Committee Of Commonalities can advise their local community as well as the Israeli and Palestinian

Governments at the federal level of the need for a peaceful solution to the Israeli-Palestinian Conflict.

Chapter 14: A Realistic Two-State Solution

I do have to apologize beforehand as I will not discuss the Golan Heights as it is a matter between Israel and Syria, and I am less familiar with Syria. I will though discuss the West Bank and pre-1967 Israel as it pertains to both the Israelis and Palestinians, a subject I know much about and am passionate about. What is pre-1967 Israel? During the Six Day War of June 1967, Israel ended up winning a war against Egypt, Syria, and Jordan. Israel came out of that war with its original borders, at least the post-1948 borders (the War Of Independence for Israel was in 1948), along with the military gains of Gaza from Egypt, East Jerusalem and the West Bank from Jordan, the Golan Heights from Syria, and the Sinai Peninsula, which was also from Egypt. Israel withdrew from the Sinai Peninsula in 1982 and gave it back to Egypt, in exchange for a Peace Treaty. Israel withdrew from Gaza in 2005.

I support what I call a realistic Two-State Solution. Israel would withdraw from The West Bank, while East Jerusalem would become a joint capitol for the Israelis and Palestinians. The West Bank and Gaza would fall under complete Palestinian control. Regular Israeli bus and

Israeli train service would help Palestinians go from Gaza to the West Bank and vice versa, with Israeli military and Israeli police protecting the busses and trains. East Jerusalem's Muslim quarter would be part of the capitol of Palestine, and the Jewish quarter would become part of the capital of Israel. Israelis who wish to remain in the West Bank would be considered Israeli Citizens living abroad in the country of Palestine, while Palestinians who wish to reside in Israel would be considered Citizens of Palestine living abroad in Israel. The Muslim quarter of East Jerusalem, while being part of the capital of Palestine, would be staffed by both Israeli Muslims and Palestinian Muslims, as a way to show friendship and peace. The Jewish quarter would be staffed by Israeli Jews from Israel. The Christian quarter would be staffed by Israeli Christians and Palestinian Christians and would be split between Israel and Palestine, in terms of responsibility. And the Armenian quarter would be staffed by Armenians, with the Armenians deciding whether they want their quarter to be part of Israel, Palestine, or both.

I feel that this is the most realistic solution to the issue at hand. Israel and Palestine would coordinate water usage in the Jordan Valley, which would be under Palestinian control, in exchange for Israel offering technological innovations and gas from offshore off of Israel's coast near the city of Haifa. In addition to having a realistic Two-State Solution, Israel would have an embassy in the original capital of Palestine, Ramallah, and Palestine would have an embassy in the Israeli city of Tel Aviv. This would lead to full diplomatic relations. After full diplomatic relations are created between Israel and Palestine, other Arab nations will follow Palestine's suit and start establishing relations with Israel. The Governmental relations between Israel and Palestine will also lead to security cooperation, which will be discussed in the two chapters after the next one.

Chapter 15: A Fair Compromise For Israel and Palestine

In exchange for agreeing to the Two-State Solution, the United States should give Palestine several M1A1 Abrams tanks, several armored Humvees, and several transport helicopters as well as Apache attack helicopters. This will help Palestine with future security needs and will help it work as part of a Middle Eastern version of NATO, which will help the Middle East as a whole. To keep its quantitative and qualitative edge in the Middle East, in exchange for agreeing to the Two-State Solution, the United States should give Israel two Los Angeles Class Attack Submarines to replace two of their German-built diesel submarines. The U.S. should also give Israel ten F-22 fighter jets to replace ten of their aging F-16 fighter jets. Israel and Palestine can then coordinate security activities together while part of a peace pact which will lead to a Middle Eastern version of NATO, to be discussed in the next chapter.

Chapter 16: A Middle Eastern Version Of NATO

In the First World War, we had the Allied Powers and the Central Powers. The Allied Powers, led by France, Great Britain, and the United States, defeated the Central Powers. Then came World War II. In the Second World War, we had the Allies and the Axis Powers. After the defeat of Nazi Germany by the Allies, led by The U.S., Great Britain, and the Soviet Union, and the defeat of Japan, the Cold War came about with the Soviet Union on one side and The United States and NATO (North Atlantic Treaty Organization) on the other side. Even after the end of the Cold War and the fall of the Berlin Wall, NATO remained in place.

I feel that the relationship between the U.S and NATO is strong and NATO countries have helped the U.S. greatly, with countries like Great Britain, Germany, among others, helping us out in the War On Terrorism. I have to say that the NATO system works well. That is why I am proposing a Middle Eastern version of NATO.

Starting with what I call the IPCISO (Israeli-Palestinian Counterterrorism and Intelligence Sharing Organization). It can be either an Office within the Senior Staff of Israeli and Palestinian Military and Government or it can be a joint unit, Special Operations or Regular Military, of the Israeli Defense Force and the Palestinian security organizations. This Office will eventually grow to form a joint Military-wide unit of Israelis and Palestinians. What I mean is this will be a two country Middle Eastern NATO. After a Peace Process deal is finalized, or even before, this Middle Eastern version of NATO may one day become greater in scope, encompassing some, most, or all of the Middle East.

Chapter 17: NASWAA

The name is not as important as the function, but I would personally name the new NATO of the Middle East as the North African-Southwest Asian Alliance (NASWAA). They would coordinate security-related issues with not only with each other in the Middle East, but with NATO and the United States. NASWAA would deploy troops throughout the Middle East to deal with terrorism-related incidents and perhaps to keep the peace as well. They would also, with approval of NATO and the U.S., for the first time, deploy outside the Middle East to help with any tensions outside the region, while partnered with NATO.

Through cooperation between countries such as Morocco, Tunisia, Libya, Algeria, Egypt, Saudi Arabia, Oman, Yemen, Qatar, Bahrain, United Arab Emirates, Turkey, Israel and Palestine, among others, these countries will work with NATO and the U.S. for security not only in the Middle East, but around the world. This would give the countries of the Middle East more presence on the world stage which would be a morale booster to their people, in my opinion. The people of these countries will feel more valued if they have more of an impact on a global level.

This will probably not come to fruition for another ten or twenty years from when I am writing this book (in 2018). We may not have a Middle Eastern NATO just yet, but we can achieve Israeli and Palestinian peace and have an Israeli-Palestinian IPCISO (Israeli-Palestinian Counterterrorism and Intelligence Sharing Organization), which will of course serve as a forerunner to the new NASWAA (North African-Southwest Asian Alliance).

Chapter 18: What It All Means

What I have now proposed in the last few chapters is a Two-State Solution, followed by more military aid for both a smaller and more secure Israel and a smaller and more secure Palestine. I have also proposed the North African-Southwest Asian Alliance, a Middle Eastern version of NATO. Once the Israelis and Palestinians have peace, and Israel is given a slight qualitative and quantitative edge for security purposes, and Palestine is given more military aid for its own internal security, they can work on security cooperation. They can work on counterterrorism operations together, they can work on intelligence sharing, and they can work on what their vision of a Middle Eastern NATO would look like.

As I am writing this, the President of the United States Mr. Donald Trump is proposing a Space Force. I am in agreement with this idea. I feel that as countries like Russia have a joint Air and Space Force, the United States should also have a Space Force. We need a Middle Eastern NATO by the year 2030. In 2030, it will operate throughout the Middle East. By 2040, it should operate throughout the world in conjunction with the European NATO and with help and support from the United States. By 2050 and 2060, we should have a joint Middle Eastern Space Command, not necessarily a space force, but a space command, that will be staffed by members of all countries of the Middle East. This will be similar to how Europe has a European Space Agency. In this fashion, the Middle East will be considered a Global Leader, along with the U.S., the U.N., the EU, and NATO countries.

Chapter 19: Why This Would Be Good For U.S. National Security And U.S. Geostrategic Goals

A Two-State Solution, with an Israel and Palestine with clear, defined borders, clear, defined militaries, clear, defined economic cooperation, and clear, defined security cooperation, would be good for the United States. It would create a domino effect in terms of international peace movements. North and South Korea may reunite to form a united Korean Peninsula. India and Pakistan may make peace. And Israel and Iran may even one day achieve peace with each other.

Giving Palestine military technology from the United States would allow its leadership to keep the peace in their country. Giving Israel a slight qualitative and quantitative edge by giving it F-22s and Los Angeles Class Submarines would insure that even a smaller Israel would remain secure.

And finally, not only would our (the U.S.'s) oil supply become more secure with less volatility in the oil market, but we would be able to eventually withdraw all troops from Iraq and Afghanistan within the next five to ten years from when I am writing this (2018). We would then also be able to remove about, let's say, 25% to 30% of U.S. Troops from the Middle East and allow for those troops to be moved to places like Eastern Europe and East Asia, which are seeing a rise in the possibility of larger conflicts forming, as in the conflict between pro-Russian separatists and Ukraine and the North and South Korea conflict possibly becoming greater in scope.

Chapter 20: Me Personally

As I sit at home writing this, I feel that Middle East peace is possible. I know I am just a simple former Army Admin Clerk and Bachelor's Degree level University graduate. But having said this, I feel that the plans laid out in this book may very well work. If they are put in place and succeed, then my service in Kuwait may make me one of the last million or so Americans (Operation Iraqi Freedom and Operation Enduring Freedom Veterans) to have served in a major campaign in the Middle East. Many more will serve in the Middle East but not in as great of a number as in Iraqi Freedom and Enduring Freedom, I hope. In the future, if plans like mine are put in place, then the Middle East will be a more peaceful place and we could very well focus on other regions of the world, security-wise, like I said in the previous chapter about U.S. National Security interests.

Conclusion

With my military experience, my time spent in the Middle East, and with my Political Science studies, I have realized that governments can and do talk to each other.

But now, it's time for the people to talk to each other. NGOs/Nonprofits should help everyday people, both in Israel and in the Palestinian territories, speak to each other. They should give everyday people a voice in the Peace Process, for it is the people that live through war and live through peace as well. I firmly believe that governments should talk to each other and the people should talk to each other. We all have differences and we, all of us, have at least one thing in common. The people should also talk to their governments to affect change, and governments should ask their people how they would like to see change as well.

A durable peace is necessary for both the Israelis and Palestinians. This conflict is not sustainable. I have to reiterate this again. This conflict is not sustainable. If the Middle East wants peace and to put themselves on a global stage, then they need to fight for peace. We need to see a Two-State Solution within the next ten or twenty years, that way, Israel and the Palestinians would be able to create joint partnerships, such as a Middle Eastern version of NATO, which could spread to include other Middle Eastern countries, and this would make the Middle East, to include Israel and Palestine, a global leader, along with the U.S. and other U.N. Security Council Members. But this will take time. I foresee something like this happening not today or tomorrow. But in one or two decades' time. The key, though, is that the work I have proposed has to start today. It has to start now. If we start now, we will have the Middle Eastern Space Command by the year 2050 or 2060.

This would be good for U.S. National Security interests because this would allow for the U.S. to transfer military and political resources to other parts of the world other than the Middle East. Parts of the world that are seeing a rise in tensions. I personally feel that peace in the Middle East would allow for us to have less future military involvement in the Middle East which would lead to more involvement in other, even more volatile regions of the World.

As a final note, I will reiterate again that we should remember that everyone has at least one thing that they all have in common with someone else, no matter how different we may seem. And I will always remember my time in Kuwait, Qatar, and Israel. That I will never forget for it gave me hope for peace in the region.

Thank you for reading this book. Take care now.

About Me, The Author

I, Vitaliy Balin, served in the U.S. Army Reserve, including a deployment to Kuwait. I have a Bachelor's Degree in Political Science which gives me a passion for politics, Middle Eastern politics in particular. I also like Middle Eastern history. In fact, one of my favorite books is The Epic Of Gilgamesh, a book written in ancient Mesopotamia, more specifically, Babylon, now known as Iraq. When I'm not at work or studying current and historical events, I like to watch science fiction movies and science fiction television shows. My two favorite sports to watch are Boxing and Mixed Martial Arts. I occasionally play video games too, but not nearly as much as I used to.

Introduction To Jerusalem 2100 AD

This book will serve as a follow-up to my previous book, *Kuwait, Qatar, And Israel*. It will discuss the Middle East from the year 2018 AD through 2100 AD. I will speak about why I support a Two-State Solution, why Israel and Palestine need security guarantees from the United States, the need for a Middle Eastern NATO, why peace would be good for U.S. strategic long term goals, and a Middle Eastern Space Command, among other ideas going into the future. I will even introduce what I call The Conservative To Liberal Approach To Governing A Country.

Chapter 1: Israel And Palestine In 2025 AD

2025 AD is the date I set as a deadline for the Israelis and Palestinians to achieve a just settlement and acquire a Two-State Solution and end their conflict permanently. Some may disagree with me and say that a One-State Solution is needed. The problem with a One-State Solution is the logistics. Israel and Palestine should be separate states and not one big state because it would be easier to manage a smaller and more secure Israel for the Israeli Government and it would be easier for the Palestinians to manage a smaller and more secure Palestine. As I am writing this (in 2018), Mahmoud Abbas is the President of the Palestinian Authority. Benjamin Netanyahu is the Prime Minister of Israel. Just based on these last two sentences, we already have a framework for peace. We already have a Palestinian Authority that can be put in charge of both Gaza and The West Bank in case a Palestinian State is established, which I feel it should be established by the year 2025 AD. We already have an Israeli cabinet with proper infrastructure that will continue to lead an already existing Israel when a Palestinian State is created.

To create a One-State Solution, we would need to combine the governing bodies of Israel and Palestine into one unit. We would then also have to combine the military and infrastructure spending of both countries into one unit. We would then have to draft an entirely new Peace Treaty and an entirely new agreement on borders. This will cost both the Israelis and Palestinians so much money. So you can see, this money can be used instead to help both of their peoples. This is why I support a Two-State Solution.

How would I formulate a Two-State Solution? I would have Gaza and The West Bank be part of the Palestinian State while Israel would have full control of Pre-1967 Israel. Israel already withdrew from the Gaza strip in 2005 and all that is really left is to withdraw from The West Bank. No withdrawal from East Jerusalem is necessary as whoever is in East Jerusalem, whether Jewish, Christian, Muslim, or Armenian, will stay in East Jerusalem. First and foremost, we need an Israeli withdrawal from The West Bank. The negotiations on East Jerusalem will come later. But I personally believe, like I stated in my last book, *Kuwait, Qatar, And Israel*, that East Jerusalem should become a capital of both Israel and Palestine. I will expand on my previous idea that I put in my last book.

Israel and Palestine would share East Jerusalem. The Christian Quarter would be jointly shared and staffed by both Israel and Palestine, with Israeli and Palestinian Christians overseeing the Christian Holy Sites. Israel would oversee the Jewish Holy Sites like The Wailing Wall. Palestine would oversee the Muslim Holy Sites. I have to add one thing I did not mention in my previous book. Israel would have complete control of The Wailing Wall on the condition that Israeli Muslims and Christians and Palestinian Muslims and Christians would also be able to pray at the Wailing Wall the way Israeli Jews and Jews worldwide are able to do. Palestine would have complete control of what is known to Muslims as The Noble Sanctuary and known to Jews as The Temple Mount on the condition that Israeli Jews and Jews worldwide would be able to pray inside of it the way Muslims and Christians would be allowed to pray at the Wailing Wall. Like I stated in my previous book, the Armenian Quarter would continue to be staffed by Armenians and would be either part of Israel, Palestine, or both, depending on the Armenians' discretion.

Israelis would live in pre-1967 Israel and Palestinians would live in the State Of Palestine, in Gaza and The West Bank. Israeli settlers who wish to remain in The West Bank would be considered Israeli Citizens living abroad in The State Of Palestine. Palestinians who wish to live within the State Of Israel would be considered Palestinian Citizens living abroad in The State Of Israel. East Jerusalem residents would either be Israeli or Palestinian Citizens, based on whether they are Israeli or Palestinian, which is basically self-explanatory. Palestinians who wish to travel from Gaza to the West Bank and vice versa would travel on normal Israeli bus and train routes but would be escorted by Israeli Police and Israeli Military for their own safety.

Chapter 2: The Conservative To Liberal Approach To Governing A Country

Just as Israel and Palestine would become separate states, we need all of the countries in the world, which are now numbered at 195, to be separate states. Why do we need this conservative approach of having countries and not having entire continents form states? The answer is limited resources. We need a country to have a President or Prime Minister that manages the already scarce financial and natural resources that that country has. That is why the United States is not yet part of a North American Union. Why Africa is not part of An African Union. Why The Middle East is not part of a Greater Middle East Union.

We probably only have enough oil and natural gas for about 100 years or so remaining. That is why it is crucial to have smaller country units, rather than continent level countries, to share these natural resources. That is my conservative approach to governing a country. With less resources and less people to govern, each of the 195 countries can continue to manage their people efficiently.

In the year 2060 or maybe it might come later in 2100, we would have what I call the liberal approach to governing a country. As I am writing this book (in 2018), Miguel Alcubierre Moya, a Mexican Theoretical Physicist, is working on formulating equations for the Alcubierre Drive. This Drive would propel spacecraft at faster than the speed of light speeds. The country of Iran has talked about building the world's first fusion reactor. The President of the United States, Mr. Donald Trump, has talked about creating a U.S. Space Force to be the Sixth Branch of the U.S. Military. The Space Force is to come to fruition in the year 2020 AD.

All of these technological innovations, such as faster than light speed, nuclear fusion, and the U.S. Space Force, will lead to us having more energy resources. Nuclear fusion would give us much more energy than we already have, if not near-unlimited energy. The Alcubierre Drive will let us travel faster in space and then mine asteroids and meteors, and send the mineral resources we harvest back to Earth. The Space Force will be another addition to the already existing NASA and other space organizations on Earth which will give us more drive and motivation to explore space. Then when we harvest near-unlimited energy, either in the 2060's AD or the 2100's AD, it will be easier for leaders to govern larger swaths of land more efficiently due to more resources being available for more people. We would then be able to have a North American Union consisting of Canada, The United States, and Mexico, an African Union, a Middle Eastern Union, a European Union which would include Russia, and an Asian Union.

Chapter 3: Security Guarantees For Israel And Palestine

By now, in this book, we are talking about the year 2025 AD, and Israel and Palestine have agreed to the Two-State Solution and are now living side by side as brothers and sisters in peace. We, The United States, need to ensure security guarantees for both sides. I will expand on my earlier comments from my book *Kuwait, Qatar, And Israel*. In that book, I mentioned giving Palestine several U.S. tanks, Humvees, and helicopters, and giving Israel two Los Angeles Class Submarines and ten F-22 fighter jets. By 2025 AD, I hypothesize that the U.S. would already have mostly stealth fighter jets even more advanced than the F-22 and its submarine fleet will be far more advanced than the existing Los Angeles Class Submarines. And its tanks, helicopters, and Humvees would be faster, stronger, more resistant to damage, and stealthier.

That is why I feel that it would not hurt U.S. National Security by giving Israel and Palestine double the technology that I proposed in my last book. For its own internal security, I would give The Palestinian Authority of Palestine ten M1A1 Abrams Tanks, thirty armored Humvees, and fifteen Apache helicopters, as well as many troop transport helicopters and armored troop transport carrier vehicles. I would give Israel five Los Angeles Class Submarines to replace their fleet of five diesel German-built submarines and I would give Israel twenty F-22 fighter jets. I would also give Israel twenty M1A1 Abrams Tanks.

The steps outlined in the previous paragraphs of this chapter would ensure both domestic security for Palestine and a slight quantitative and qualitative edge for Israel, thereby giving both countries a sense of internal security as well as external security for the Israelis. By the year 2030, the Israelis and Palestinians can form joint intelligence and security-sharing partnerships, which will lead the Middle East to have a greater security-sharing partnership like Europe's NATO. NATO has worked successfully to counteract The Soviet Union for many decades as well and that is why it is a good model for the Middle East to follow. NATO also functioned well in The War On Terrorism, and that is yet another reason for it to be used as a model for the Middle East.

Chapter 4: Israel And Palestine In 2030 AD

Israel and Palestine would increase security cooperation by 2030 AD. They would convince all armed non-government factions such as Hezbollah and Hamas to disarm as there is peace between Israel and Palestine and no need for further fighting. They would have a two country security cooperation which would lead to a greater security cooperation in all of North Africa, The Arabian Peninsula, Turkey, and Iran.

Initially, since relations in 2018 AD are improving between Israel and Saudi Arabia, I feel that Israel, Palestine, and the Arabian Peninsula states will form a joint security pact in 2030 AD. This Israeli-Palestinian-Arabian Peninsula Pact will then negotiate with Iran to not work on nuclear weapons capabilities, but instead to focus only on peaceful nuclear energy, such as the fusion reactor the Iranian leadership stated that it is working on. The UN, The U.S., and the Arabian Peninsula countries, and Israel and Palestine will oversee Iranian nuclear development and ensure that it is peaceful. Iran then will work together with this Israeli-Palestinian-Arabian Peninsula Pact to create peace in places like Yemen, which are seeing a rise in hostilities in 2018 AD.

Chapter 5: The Middle East On A Global Stage In 2040 AD

By the year 2040 AD, Israel and Palestine will form a joint security pact with not only the Arabian Peninsula, but with Iran, Turkey, and the North African States.

Turkey will have the distinction of being the first NATO member to be part of both this Middle Eastern Alliance and NATO as well.

I feel that this will definitely give the Middle Eastern countries more standing on the World Stage. During the Cold War, most of the Middle Eastern countries were considered non-aligned nation-states. I feel that a Middle Eastern NATO would help bring about a change in world opinion. Middle Eastern countries that were once considered non-aligned will now be major decision makers, along with the U.S., The European Union, and Russia, among others.

In 2040 AD, China and Russia will become more powerful. They may very well become superpowers the way the United States is a superpower now in 2018 AD. There may very well be peaceful negotiations with Russia and China to form unions with them, such as finally brining Russia into NATO and bringing China into an Asian Union.

In one of the previous chapters, I spoke about liberal and conservative approaches to governing a country. By 2040 AD, we will be in an in-between period. We will have a period where countries will have better technology to harvest existing natural resources. This will allow for more continent-wide partnerships. Who knows, Russia may even join the European Union by 2040 AD. We will wait and see.

But just as the U.S. and other countries have given financial and military aid to the Middle East, I feel it is time for the Middle East to give back to the world at large. I feel that it is not enough for the Middle Eastern version of NATO to only patrol and secure Middle Eastern countries. By 2040 AD, the world will be even more global than it is today and the NASWAA (North African-Southwest Asian Alliance), which I will call it for the rest of the book, will go on security operations all over the world. NASWAA is the name I gave for the Middle Eastern version of NATO in my previous book, *Kuwait, Qatar, And Israel*.

Chapter 6: Eastern Europe And East Asia In 2040 AD

We, the United States, may not yet have a complete working relationship with Russia and China in 2040 AD. We may yet have some disagreements. By 2040 AD, Russia and China may become superpowers like the U.S. is currently a superpower. That is why NATO and the NASWAA may very well have to deploy to Eastern Europe and East Asia, for security reasons. In 2018 AD, there are battles in Eastern Ukraine between Pro-Russian separatists and the Ukrainian Government. In East Asia, in 2018 AD, there is still conflict between North and South Korea.

We should encourage Russia to convince the Pro-Russian separatists to lay down their arms, and we should encourage Russia to give back the Crimean Peninsula to Ukraine, and in exchange, Ukraine will work with The European Union, Russia, and the United States for a peaceful solution. And in the future, Ukraine may very well work with The European Union, Russia, and the United States, all on equal terms, to avoid conflict with any of the three. This is how we would avoid any future conflicts with Russia.

In East Asia, North and South Korea are still in conflict. I support Mr. Trump's steps in negotiating peace between the two countries of the Korean Peninsula. Also, China is becoming stronger, both financially and militarily. In order to avoid conflict with China in the year 2040 AD, I feel we need to support Mr. Trump's steps in negotiating for better trade deals. All of these steps I mentioned in this paragraph and the previous paragraph will help prevent future wars around the year 2040 AD and will lead to even a superpower Russia and superpower China to live peacefully with the superpower United States.

The NASWAA countries of course, along with NATO, in the near-term, around 2030 AD or so, will of course have to deploy to Eastern Europe and East Asia to help secure U.S. and NATO interests there. But by 2040 AD, hopefully there will be peace in Eastern Europe and East Asia.

Chapter 7: U.S. National Security Goals And The NASWAA In 2040 AD

By 2040 AD, the NASWAA is formed and is going on security missions all over the world. No longer are non-aligned nations of the Middle East non-aligned, but are global leaders on the world stage. I said in my previous book, *Kuwait, Qatar, And Israel*, that Israel and Kuwait only have a few skyscrapers in Tel Aviv and Kuwait City, respectively, and smaller concrete buildings everywhere else, but this will change in 2040 AD. In 2040 AD, there will be many Dubai-style hotels that are thousands of feet tall throughout the Middle East. There will be many monorails and anti-gravity trains, anti-gravity busses, and anti-gravity cars, as well as flying cars. For those of you that haven't read my previous book, *Kuwait, Qatar, And Israel,* I want to make a confession. I am scared of heights. In the future, buildings will mostly be thousands of feet tall and there will be flying cars. But in the future, we will probably have pills or therapies that cure the fear of heights. So by 2040 AD, I will probably have nothing to fear.

Peace in the Middle East would create, by 2025 AD and 2030 AD, a more stable and more secure oil supply, which will work for the U.S. in the short and intermediate term, until more near-unlimited forms of energy are created. Having a stable NASWAA that not only patrols its own borders in the Middle East, but patrols the whole world, with the help of NATO and the U.S., only strengthens both U.S. and Middle Eastern security positions. It strengthens U.S. positions in that it shows that we can partially exit the Middle East to deal with conflicts that are boiling elsewhere. It strengthens Middle East positions in that the Middle East will, in general, have a greater position on the world stage. By 2040 AD, The U.S. and the NASWAA will have an equal position on the world stage, along with China and Russia, and The European Union.

Chapter 8: The Middle Eastern Space Command In 2060 AD

Just like the United States has NASA, and Europe has a European Space Agency, the NASWAA should have its own Space Command. Headquartered in Tel Aviv, Algiers, and Baghdad, it will have three headquarters initially and will send astronauts into space. By 2060 AD, countries like Iran and Israel and Palestine will have some of the greatest space launching capabilities known to humanity.

By 2060 AD, the NASWAA, the UN, NATO, and the U.S., will have by now worked for many decades with Iran on peaceful nuclear energy development. By the same year, Iran and Israel, the U.S., India, China, and Russia would have developed some of the world's first nuclear fusion plants. These plants will provide near unlimited energy. This will allow the world to work on better shuttle and rocket programs for space travel.

Former adversaries, now friends, Israeli and Iranian scientists will go into space together. India and Pakistan, inspired by the Israeli-Palestinian Peace Process and success of it, will send astronauts into space together. A united Korean Peninsula will send astronauts to space together.

Chapter 9: A Conservative Approach To Nation-States Gives Way To A Liberal Approach To Nation-States in 2100 AD And Beyond

By 2100 AD, we will have the Space Forces of the world as not at the forefront of fighting wars on Earth, but of stopping threats from outside the planet like rogue asteroids. By 2100 AD, nuclear fusion will become the primary source of power for the planet. We will then have more energy for more people. Countries will soon become partnerships on a continental scale that will not fight but will compete with each other to see who can make the future even brighter first. The Middle East will have a partnership which will be called The Middle Eastern Union. Mexico, Canada, and The United States will have a North American Union. The already existing European Union will now include Ukraine and Russia, living together in peace. East Asia will have an East Asian Union to include China and a United Korea. Conservative approaches to countries will give way to liberal approaches to countries. We will now go down from 195 countries to seven continents. Each continent will have one President and one Congress, based on the Original U.S. Constitution, signed in 1776 AD.

By 2200 AD, we may very well have the Alcubierre Drive functioning and we may be able to go at faster than light speeds and harvest mineral resources from asteroids. Unlimited fusion power and mineral resources from asteroids will give us the ability to create a world government in 2300 AD. This Government may be called the United Nations still, and it will be given more power, or it may be something different altogether.

Chapter 10: Jerusalem In 2100 AD And Beyond

By now, in 2100 AD, most countries in the world have now formed closer economic and security partnerships and are now working at the continent level. Israel and Palestine, which started as a Two-State Solution, is now a One State Peninsula, and part of a Greater Middle East. Jerusalem will, as it always was, be a welcoming place for Jews, Christians, and Muslims.

But by now, we will have even more liberal interpretations of religion as space travel becomes more routine. And by 2200 AD and 2300 AD, we will have colonies on Mars as well as outside our solar system, by at least several light years away from Earth. By the way, a light year is 6 trillion miles and the Milky Way Galaxy is 100,000 light years across.

Conclusion

From a Two-State Solution to the Israeli-Palestinian conflict, to the entire world exploring space, this book covered the story of what I think will happen not just in the Middle East from 2018 AD through 2100 AD and beyond, but what will happen in the entire world through 2100 AD and beyond. We will have Middle East Peace, eventually followed by continental and then global partnerships. We will then set out to explore space where former adversaries will travel both inside and outside the solar system, now as brothers and sisters.

Author Information

I, Vitaliy Balin, have a passion for Military History, Politics (especially Middle Eastern politics), watching Mixed Martial Arts, watching Boxing, and Science Fiction television. These are all things that I like and am passionate about.

9 781718 180352